I0002193

Microsoft Access Tutorial Guide

The Definitive User Manual To Master Access with Illustrations

By

Isaac Alejo

Table of Content

INTRODUCTION

You might have encountered situations where you must apply it professionally or oversee a charitable endeavor. Access to a tool that helps you organize your information becomes essential in these scenarios and for individuals managing extensive personal contacts and commitments. This tool allows you to swiftly find names or transactions with a few keyboard inputs, eliminating spending valuable time scrolling through spreadsheets or navigating smartphone apps. It's also valuable for creating user-friendly forms that streamline data entry for your team and ensure the accuracy and usefulness of the entered data. To effectively manage the considerable volume of information you possess, having Access is a necessity.

CHAPTER 1: NAVIGATING THE ACCESS WORKSPACE

Getting started

Starting Access is a straightforward process with multiple options, accommodating various scenarios. You can launch the application in different ways. You can access the necessary tools immediately, whether you want to view and edit an existing Access database or create a new one.

To open an existing database, you can double-click its name in the File Explorer window or use an icon on your desktop. Alternatively, you can start Access from the Start menu or taskbar (if pinned) and then choose the existing database you want to work with. Starting a new blank database from scratch or using one of the Access templates are also available options.

If you opened Access from the Start menu or a desktop/taskbar icon and wish to open an existing database, you can use the Open command in the left panel. This command allows you to access recently used databases or browse for one. The options under the Open command include:

- **Recent:** Displays a list of recently used files and folders, allowing quick Access to any of the listed Recent Databases.

- **Sites:** Opens a selected folder in your SharePoint server.

- **Personal:** For those with a personal Office subscription, there is also an option for Personal OneDrive.

- **This PC:** Provides a list of database files found in the last folder where you saved an Access database. If this is your first time saving an Access database, it takes you to the default Documents folder.

- **Add a Place:** This allows you to add SharePoint and OneDrive locations.

- **Browse:** Opens an Open dialog box for navigating to the drive and folder containing the desired database.

You can start Access in various ways, such as from the Start menu, desktop, taskbar, or File Explorer. Once you begin working, the onscreen tools become accessible, offering a comprehensive overview of the Access workspace, including various views, features, and buttons.

Working with Onscreen Tools in Access

When you open a database, whether an existing one or a new one starting from scratch or a template, the workspace transforms, presenting the Ribbon with its tabs: Home, Create, External Data, Database Tools, and Help.

It's essential to note that these tabs are distinct from the context-sensitive tabs that appear when you create or edit different database objects, such as tables, forms, queries, or reports within your database.

Clicking tabs

To switch between tabs on the Ribbon, click on the tab's name. It's easy to identify the currently open tab; the Create tab stands out with all its buttons visible. It brightens when you hover over another tab, but its buttons remain hidden until you click it.

Once you create an object, such as a table, clicking "Table" on the Create tab automatically displays the Table Fields tab. Access is aware of your actions within the application and presents the relevant tab based on what you've just done.

Using buttons

Access buttons can be categorized into two types:

- **Buttons that act upon clicking:** These buttons can open dialog boxes wizards or execute specific changes or tasks within your open table, report, query, or form.

- **Buttons representing lists or menus of choices:** This category has two subtypes:

- **Drop-down list buttons:** These buttons have a small, down-pointing triangle next to them on the right side. When you click the triangle, a list of options is displayed.

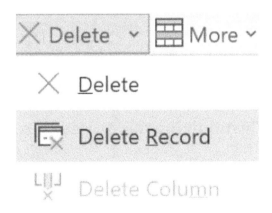

- **Buttons with a down-pointing triangle at the bottom:** Some buttons have this triangle at the bottom. A menu with additional choices appears when you click the bottom half of the button (or the triangle itself).

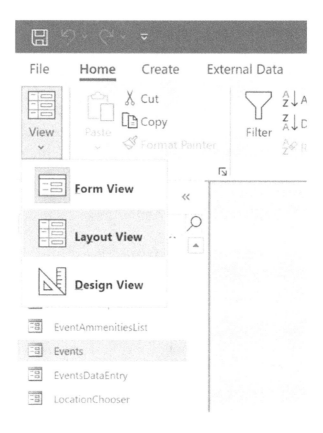

Customizing the Access Workspace

Like any good software application, Access allows users to customize their workspace to suit their preferences. This customization includes various options such as adding and rearranging buttons on the toolbar, dragging toolbars and panes to optimize layout, and making adjustments to the Quick Access Toolbar, Ribbon, status bar, and ScreenTips.

While Access comes with default settings that cater to the average or most common user, it understands that some users may prefer a more personalized experience. Therefore, the option to customize the workspace allows users to feel more at home and make their mark on their environment, much like how one might fluff pillows on a couch before lying down. However, it's important to note that customization is not necessary, as the default settings are designed to be user-friendly and practical.

Repositioning the Quick Access Toolbar

You have two options for the position of the Quick Access Toolbar:

- The default location is above the Ribbon.

- You can also choose to place it below the Ribbon.

Right-click the Quick Access Toolbar and select "Show Quick Access Toolbar Below the Ribbon" from the pop-up menu to move it. Alternatively, clicking the down-pointing triangle at the right end of the Quick Access Toolbar also offers the "Show Below the Ribbon" command.

If you decide to place the Quick Access Toolbar below the Ribbon, you'll notice that the same command (accessible by right-clicking the toolbar in its new position) changes to "Show Quick Access Toolbar Above the Ribbon." It toggles between the two options depending on its current location. However, I don't recommend moving it from its default location above the Ribbon, as it's more convenient and user-friendly when separate from the main workspace and Ribbon tabs.

Remember that you don't have to right-click the Quick Access Toolbar to reposition it precisely. When you right-click the tabs, the "Show ..." command is also available in the pop-up menu.

Adding buttons to the Quick Access Toolbar

To add commands to the Quick Access Toolbar in Access, you can access the customization options in various ways. Here's how you can do it:

1. With any database open and the Ribbon tabs displayed, right-click any button on any of the tabs to initiate the customization process.

    You can also right-click the Quick Access Toolbar or Ribbon tab to access the customization options.

2. Choose "Customize Quick Access Toolbar," and the Access Options dialog box will open, displaying the customization options for the Quick Access Toolbar.

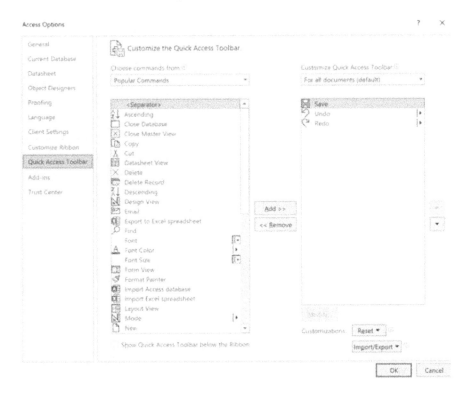

3. Select a command category in the "Choose Commands From" drop-down list. By default, a list of "Popular Commands" is displayed.

4. From the chosen category, click on the commands you want to see on the Quick Access Toolbar and click the "Add" button. The selected commands will be added to the list on the right.

5. You can use the up and down-pointing triangles on the right side of the list to reorder the added commands, determining their left-to-right appearance on the toolbar.

Continue selecting categories and commands from the left and clicking "Add" to include them in the list on the right.

Note that not all commands will always be available on the Quick Access Toolbar. For example, adding the "Filter" button from the Home tab will only be usable when a table or set of query results is open.

- After adding all the desired commands, click "OK" to apply the changes and close the dialog box. The Quick Access Toolbar will expand to accommodate the newly added buttons.

If you want to add a specific button to the Quick Access Toolbar and can see the button you want to add, right-click the button and choose "Add to Quick Access Toolbar" from the menu. The selected button will instantly appear on the toolbar, staying within the tab where it was located when you right-clicked it.

The Access Options dialog box allows you to select buttons from all the various tabs in one place, eliminating the need to search for the buttons you want to add. However, the right-click method is more efficient if you only need to add a single visible button now. It's a matter of preference and convenience, depending on the situation.

Removing buttons from the Quick Access Toolbar

Need to remove a command from the Quick Access Toolbar? It's a simple process:

1. Please hover over the unwanted button on the Quick Access Toolbar and right-click it.

2. From the pop-up menu, choose "Remove from Quick Access Toolbar."

   Voilà! The command is now gone from the Quick Access Toolbar.

Don't worry; the button isn't lost; it remains on the tab where it originally resided. It just no longer occupies space at the top of the Access workspace.

Minimizing the Ribbon

Need more space to work? If you want to spread out and have more workspace in Access, you can minimize the Ribbon, reducing it to just a strip with the tab titles visible (showing whichever tabs are currently open). The minimized Ribbon can be quickly restored to its full size when needed.

To minimize the Ribbon, follow these steps:

1. Right-click anywhere on the Ribbon.

    A pop-up menu will appear. You can right-click a button, a Ribbon tab, or a group name (such as "Reports" on the Create tab or "Text Formatting" on the Home tab), and the appropriate pop-up menu will be displayed.

2. Choose "Collapse the Ribbon."

    The Ribbon will be reduced to a long bar containing only the tab titles. You can still access any tab and temporarily display its buttons by clicking on the tab with your mouse.

3. To restore the Ribbon to its full size, right-click the minimized Ribbon and again choose "Collapse the Ribbon." The command will now be checked, indicating that the Ribbon is currently minimized. Clicking the

command to reselect it will toggle this setting off, and the Ribbon will return to its full size.

Working with ScreenTips

ScreenTips in Access are small descriptions that appear when you hover your mouse pointer over onscreen tools such as buttons, commands, and menus, providing names and brief explanations of their functions within the workspace.

While not all onscreen features have ScreenTips, anything that can be clicked to act, open a dialog box, or create something usually has associated ScreenTips that you can choose to view or hide. If you opt to see them, you can select between concise or more detailed tips.

To customize Access's ScreenTips settings, follow these steps:

1. Click the File tab and the File menu (the red panel on the far left), and the Info view will appear on the workspace.

2. Click the Options command near the bottom of the menu to open the Access Options dialog box.

3. From the list on the left side of the dialog box, choose "General." The options related to ScreenTips, file formats, folders, and name initials will be displayed.

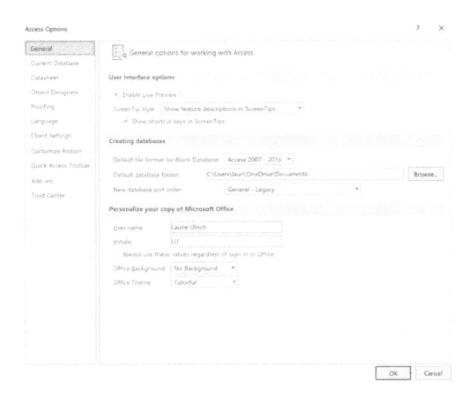

4. In the first section of the dialog box, click the ScreenTip Style drop-down list.

5. Select from the following options:

- **Show Feature Descriptions in ScreenTips:** This choice provides ScreenTips with additional information. It includes the button name and briefly describes its function or effect. It may also offer links to more assistance and information.

Navigation Pane

- **Don't Show Feature Descriptions in ScreenTips:** Opt for this option if you prefer straightforward ScreenTips showing only the button name without further explanations.

- **Don't Show ScreenTips:** If you prefer to work without ScreenTips altogether, choose this option to disable them.

6. Click OK to close the Access Options dialog box, and your ScreenTips settings will be updated accordingly.

Mousing Around

Access offers some support for this approach if you prefer using the keyboard extensively while working with software. However, it would help if you used a specific key to make the keyboard function as a commander.

Press the Alt key to switch between tabs and issue commands using the keyboard. When you do this, you'll notice numbers and letters appearing in small squares on the Quick Access Toolbar and the Ribbon's tabs,

Once these characters are visible, you can press the corresponding key on your keyboard to execute a command (for example, pressing 1 to Save) or switch to a specific tab (like pressing C to access the Create tab).

When you are on a tab (activated by pressing its letter key), the buttons on that tab will display their respective keyboard shortcuts. However, you will see key combinations, such as F+Z (shown as FZ onscreen) instead of single numbers or letters, to activate the Form Wizard.

Navigating Access with the Alt Key

For those who prefer using the keyboard extensively while working with software, Access offers some degree of support for this approach. However, there is a catch: a specific key must be used to enable keyboard commanding.

Press the Alt key to switch between tabs and issue commands using the keyboard instead of the mouse. Upon doing so, numbers and letters will appear in small squares on the Quick Access Toolbar and the Ribbon tabs. Once these characters are visible, you can press the corresponding key on your keyboard to execute a command (for instance, pressing 1 to Save) or switch to a particular tab (like pressing C to access the Create tab).

When you are on a tab (activated by pressing its letter key), the buttons on that tab will display their respective keyboard shortcuts. However, these shortcuts now involve key combinations to activate the Form Wizard, like F+Z (represented as FZ onscreen).

CHAPTER 2: DATABASE BASICS

Database Lingo

Don't be stressed by the section heading ("Database Lingo") – I'm not asking you to memorize a bunch of technical jargon. The following section and several others in this chapter introduce essential terms you need to understand to navigate Access effectively. Knowing these terms will help you comprehend the Access workspace's ribbons, dialog boxes, and various onscreen tools.

While you should know a few technical words, they are basic, and you might already be familiar with some. They include terms like "record" and "database." Understanding these concepts will enable you to grasp how the pieces fit together in the larger picture of a database.

In Access, data refers to the information it stores. How you think about and store information in your mind may differ from how a database program like Access handles it. For instance, you might think of a person's name as "John Smith," while Access stores it in separate fields like "First Name" (John) and "Last Name" (Smith). By breaking down the data into smaller pieces, you gain more flexibility and can sort and utilize the information efficiently.

To keep data organized, databases use fields to provide a home for each piece of data. Each field holds a specific type of data. For example, in a baseball card collection database, fields could include "Manufacturer," "Player Name," "Position," "Year,"

25

"Team," and "Average" (or "ERA" for pitchers). Similarly, in a name and address database, fields might include "Last Name," "First Name," "Middle Initial," "Address1," "Address2," "City," "State," "Zip," "Phone," "Cell," and "Email." Fields represent all the attributes and details you want to capture about a person, product, or any other item in your database.

As with the term data, other database programs (such as QuickBase or FileMaker) all agree on what a field is. In larger database packages, however (such as Oracle and Microsoft SQL Server), you find the term column replacing field. To make things more exciting, Microsoft Excel stores your fields in columns when you use an Excel spreadsheet to store a list. The tabular structure of a database table leads Oracle and SQL to refer to columns rather than fields, but for heaven's sake — couldn't they have stuck to a term we all know?

Records

Fields provide essential data, but to establish meaningful connections, you need something more organized - that's where records come in. A record encompasses all the fields for a specific item, like a baseball card, client, or product. In a table, each record holds the same fields but can contain different data. Not every record needs to fill every field; for instance, if someone doesn't have a cell phone, the "Cell" field would remain empty for that individual.

A table, on the other hand, is a collection of records that share similar data. It's crucial to emphasize "similar data" here. All records within a table consist of fields relevant to that particular data category. For example, you could have a table dedicated to your baseball card collection, another for clients, and one more for products. However, storing unrelated data in the same table would be impractical, just as you wouldn't store your car's repair records with your cookie recipes. Maintaining separate tables ensures clarity and efficiency, making generating queries and reports for specific data categories easier and avoiding confusion that could lead to nonsensical results.

The database

An Access database, or a database file, serves as a comprehensive repository for a specific information set. It encompasses all the tables, queries, reports, and forms created in Access to efficiently manage and interact with the data. Instead of individually storing these components on the disk drive, Access combines them into a cohesive file.

The essential point is that the database is not solely about the data; it comprises all the tools necessary to store, manipulate, and visualize it. Even before any records are entered into the tables, the database includes the components facilitating data management and analysis. In other words, it encompasses the complete suite of tools to work with the data effectively.

Field Types and Uses

Your data resides in a field, holding individual pieces of information like Last Name or Batting Average.

Given the diverse nature of information in the world, Access provides a range of field types to accommodate various data types. In essence, Access offers the following field types to cater to your specific data storage needs:

- Short Text

- Long Text

- Number

- Large Number

- Date/Time

- Date/Time Extended

- Currency

- AutoNumber (this data type is applied, by default, to the starting ID field in any new table)

- Yes/No

- OLE Object

- Attachment

- Hyperlink

- Calculated

- Lookup Wizard

The field types listed above are options for creating additional fields containing your data.

Let's focus on the AutoNumber field, which generates a unique number for each record, ensuring their individuality.

The Lookup Wizard's practical use will be discussed later in the book. This chapter will teach you more about when and how this data type is employed.

Don't worry about understanding the specifics of each field type based on its name right now. I will go through each type shortly. As you can see, the list encompasses almost any imaginable data type. Additionally, each type can be customized extensively to meet your requirements if you want to learn about modifying field specifications.

Below is an upcoming list that introduces the available field types and their respective uses. You'll also get insights into how you can customize them to suit your specific needs:

- **Short Text:** Stores up to 255 characters of text, including letters, numbers, punctuation, and their combinations.

- **Long Text:** Replacing the Memo field type in earlier versions, this field can hold up to 64,000 characters, equivalent to nearly 18 pages of text. It's ideal for comprehensive notes, detailed descriptions, and content requiring ample space.

Remember that when you enter numbers in a text field, they are treated as mere collections of digits, not as numerical values for calculations. When designing your database tables, be cautious, as you wouldn't want to store a value intended for calculations or reports as text, rendering it unusable as a number. Ensure that numeric data is stored as such.

Text fields have a crucial setting called size, indicating the number of characters the field can hold. For example, if you create a field called "First Name" with a size of 6, it can accommodate "Joseph" but not "Jennifer." A good practice is to make the field slightly larger than you anticipate needing, as it's easy to adjust later if necessary.

Now, let's get into the available field types:

- **Number:** Used for storing real numerical values, enabling mathematical calculations.

- **Large Number:** Be cautious with this type, as it may make your database incompatible with versions of Access before 2016. You'll be warned about this during application.

- **Currency:** Designed for tracking monetary values, prices, and invoice amounts.

- **AutoNumber:** Automatically generated for the ID field in new tables, providing a unique value for each record.

- **Date/Time:** Stores time, date, or a combination of both, offering versatility in tracking events.

- **Date/Time Extended:** Ideal for extreme precision in dates and times, down to milliseconds. Opt for the regular Date/Time field unless you require such high precision.

- **Yes/No:** This field type stores responses as Yes/No, True/False, or On/Off, depending on the format chosen. It's suitable for straightforward yes-or-no questions.

- **OLE Object:** With this data type, you can link or embed objects, like Excel worksheets or Word documents, to an Access table.

- **Attachment:** Use this field type to attach files, including documents, presentations, graphics, and more, to a record.

- **Hyperlink:** Access recognizes and stores special link language for Internet links, making it useful for those using Access on a network or extensively on the Internet.

- **Calculated:** When you want a field to display the result of a formula using other fields in the same table, this data type comes in handy. You set up the formula using the Expression Builder dialog box.

- **Lookup Wizard:** This option lets you create a fixed list of choices for a field, ensuring specific entry options. For example, you can set up a Size field with options like "Small," "Medium," and "Large" to prevent other values like "Huge" or "Tiny."

Another field type to consider is the Hyperlink field, which is also considered text but specifically stores URLs as URLs, not just as a regular string of text and punctuation.

If the distinction between text and numbers needs to be clarified, remember that computers treat numbers used in calculations differently from strings of digits like phone numbers. Different text fields in the database vary based on the amount of text they store and whether they require specific formatting to function correctly.

When naming fields, starting with a letter or number is wise. Although Access allows certain characters at the beginning or within field names, it's not advisable as it can confuse others using the database. Symbols can be challenging to read when the font size is small, and they might need to provide more insight into the field's content. After the first character, you may find logical uses for symbols like plus signs or underscores. Spaces are acceptable in field names as well. However, certain symbols should be avoided, as indicated.

Keep field names short and easy to comprehend, even though you have up to 64 characters for a field name. Avoid using all available space, but only create overly concise names like N1 or AZ773 if they hold specific meanings for your company or organization.

Stick to letters, numbers, and the occasional space in your field names. Access may permit various punctuation marks in field names, but simplicity ensures your Access solution is manageable.

Choosing Between Flat and Relational Databases

Databases are categorized into flat-file and relational, unlike the various flavors of ice cream. The choice between the two isn't a matter of personal preference but rather depends on the specific requirements of the database. Some databases necessitate a relational approach, while others would be too complex if approached that way. Continue reading to understand how to distinguish between the two types.

Isolationist tables

In a flat system, or a flat-file system, all the data is stored in a single table. A phone directory serves as an excellent example of a flat-file database, where names, addresses, and phone numbers are all stored together in one place. While some duplication may occur, such as listing a person's name and address multiple times for multiple phone lines, it generally doesn't cause significant issues, and the database functions effectively in this format.

Tables that mix and mingle

In a relational system, also known as a relational database, storage space is minimized by reducing duplicated or redundant data. To achieve this, the database breaks down the data into multiple tables, each holding a specific portion of the overall data.

Using the phone book example, one table in a relational database can contain customer name and address information, while another holds the phone numbers. This way, the individual with three phone lines has only one entry in the "customer" table (representing one customer) but three separate entries in the "phone number" table (each entry for a distinct phone line). This approach helps optimize data storage and reduce redundancy within the database.

The key to relational databases

The key field, also known as the linking field, plays a crucial role in the functionality of relational database systems. Every related table in the database contains this special field, and its data serves to identify matching records across different tables.

To understand the concept better, consider the key field as a claim stub you receive when dropping off your dry cleaning. When you want to pick up your dry cleaning, you present the claim check with its unique number. This number helps the clerk find and link your cleaning to you.

Similarly, in the phone book example, each customer has a unique customer ID. The "phone number" table stores the customer ID alongside each phone number. To determine who owns a phone number, look up the customer ID in the "customer name" table. Though it involves more steps than the plain flat-file system, the relational system saves storage space (by avoiding duplicate names) and reduces the likelihood of errors.

Relational databases can be complex, but Access handles most behind-the-scenes work. It empowers users without revealing the intricacies involved.

Now that you have an understanding of the distinction between flat-file and relational databases, you should consider which approach suits your database needs best:

- Flat-file systems are simple to create and maintain, much like Microsoft Excel spreadsheets. They work well for uncomplicated databases.

- Relational systems shine in more extensive business applications like invoicing, accounting, or inventory management. They become invaluable when dealing with substantial amounts of data.

Note that if you plan to build a relational database, you should seek help from someone experienced in database construction. It can be challenging, and proper guidance will increase your chances of success. Despite being a relational database program, Access also easily accommodates flat-file systems. Access remains the ideal program for your database project, whether you opt for a flat file or relational structure.

Building a Database

After familiarizing yourself with the initial chapters and references to other sections in the book, you may feel prepared to begin building your database. Take your time and follow these steps to set up a new database and create the first table using the Table Wizard:

1. Start Access if it's not running already.

    In the Access workspace, you'll see a series of large template icons below a "Search for Online Templates" box and links to likely searches for various templates.

2. Click the "Blank Database" icon to initiate creating a new database.

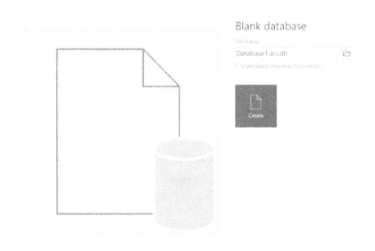

3. A "Blank Database" dialog box will appear, and you should replace the generic "DatabaseX" name with a specific name for your database.

4. If you wish to change the folder where the database will be stored, click the folder icon and choose a different location.

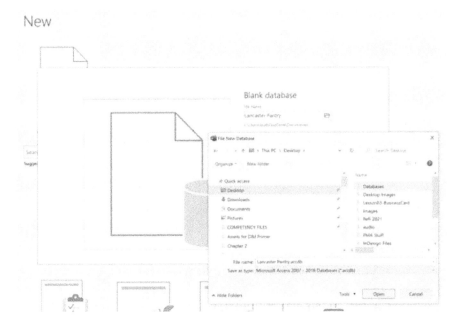

5. Click the "Create" button to proceed, and a blank table named "Table1" will appear in the central section of the workspace, along with a panel on the left that lists the parts of your database.

6. Click on "Click to Add" at the top of the second column in the table to create and name your fields.

7. Click the arrow next to "Click to Add" to select the type of field you want to add. Most fields will be of type "Short Text" by default, but choose the appropriate type based on your data and its intended use.

   Note that the first column contains an "ID" field as a unique identifier for each record. You can change its name later if necessary.

8. To name a new field, select the generic "FieldX" name (X represents a number), type a new name, and press Enter to save it.

9. Repeat steps 10 and 11 to create all the fields you need for this table. Remember that you can rename them later, so don't worry about perfection at this stage.

10. To save your new table and the entire database, press Ctrl+S or click the "Save" button on the Quick Access Toolbar. It's a good practice to save after each significant step to avoid redoing your work.

If you want to rename "Table1" to a more descriptive name:

- Right-click the Table tab.

- Choose "Save" from the pop-up menu that appears.

- Type the new table name in the resulting "Save As" dialog box.

- Click "OK" to confirm the name change.

- Resave your database to include this modification.

- Remember, "Table1" is typically not a helpful name for a table, so renaming it to something descriptive will make your database more organized and user-friendly.

Adding and Removing Tables

Even experienced experts make mistakes, such as building unnecessary tables or forgetting required ones. If you need to add or remove tables, Access's user-friendly interface allows you to do so quickly. The key is to get started, build your database, and refine it as you go along.

When adding new tables to an existing database, follow these steps for each table:

1. Click the Create tab on the Ribbon.

2. Click the Table button on the Ribbon to create a new blank table.

3. Build and name the fields for the new table.

4. Save your database periodically as you work.

5. Continue adding tables as needed.

Remember that it's okay to be flawed from the start; you can always make changes later. Properly naming tables is crucial for easy identification, so avoid generic names like Table1 or Table2. Instead, give them meaningful names like Customers, Orders, or Products. You can name a table when prompted to save it or rename it later by right-clicking the current name in the left-hand panel and typing the new one.

CHAPTER 3: SOUNDS LIKE A PLAN

Planning Your Database Tables

Tables consist of fields, the information you intend to store in your database. Hopefully, you organized your list of fields into logical groups. Have you done that? I emphasize this point because table design is a critical aspect of database creation, yet it is often overlooked. Let's either begin or retrieve your field list to proceed with the work.

Reviewing fields

Review your field list and consider how you'll utilize the data. For instance, consider "Volunteer Name" as one of your fields. You should contemplate whether it should be one field or two. Using one field is suitable if you consistently refer to volunteers by their full names. However, you may need separate fields for the first and last names in generating emails.

Similarly, for the "Address" field, consider if you want to group volunteers by city in a report. If yes, having separate fields for street, city, state, and zip/postal code provides more flexibility.

It's crucial to examine your field list and ensure that each piece of information is at the most granular level. Taking the time to think through this now will save you trouble later. When you have your "Volunteer Name" field in multiple forms and reports and later need to implement email functionality, having two fields (first name and last name) will make the process smoother, whereas using one field will require adjustments across forms and reports.

Determining data types

Once you have a well-prepared list of fields, it's essential to consider the data type that each field will hold. Will it store a date, a number, text, or maybe just binary choices like true or false? Properly setting data types significantly impacts your database's overall size and performance. Next to each field, note the data type it will contain and specify the maximum size of that data.

Text data

Access offers two data types - Long Text and Short Text. The Long Text can store up to 64,000 characters, while the Short Text can store up to 255 characters, allowing you to specify the exact number of characters using the Field Size property. The most suitable choice becomes evident once you consider the reasons behind it.

Opting for Long Text for the state field would reserve a capacity of 64,000 characters, even though you only need to store two characters. It would unnecessarily inflate the size of your database, leading to potential performance degradation over time. To avoid this, choosing Short Text with a Field Size of 2 is better, which will efficiently meet your requirements.

On the other hand, being too conservative can also cause issues. For example, setting a Short Text data type with a Field Size of 10 for the LastName field might be fine unless a volunteer has a last name that exceeds 10 characters. In such cases, Access won't allow you to input an 11-character name in that field, necessitating a change to accommodate the longest possible name. Therefore, choosing data types wisely is essential to strike the right balance between storage capacity and efficient utilization.

Number data

The guidelines for text fields also apply to numbers. It's essential to select a number field size that closely matches the size of the number you intend to store without going below it. Table 4-1 details the number of field sizes, their maximum values, and decimal places.

A significant digit refers to a non-zero number on either side of the decimal point. For instance, 0.123 has three significant digits, 22.00013 has four significant digits, and 42 has two significant digits. Single field size will accept 0.1234567 but not 12.1234567, as the former has seven significant digits while the latter has nine. The number will be rounded and truncated to fit within the Single field size.

There's also a seventh number field size called Replication ID, primarily for compatibility with older versions of Access that supported replication.

If a number won't be used for calculations, consider using one of the text data types. For instance, zip codes often begin with a zero, and using a number data type may remove the leading zero, resulting in inaccurate data. In such cases, opting for a text data type, such as Small Text with a Field Size of 9, will retain the leading zero.

Assigning data types and sizes can be complicated. When in doubt, choose a slightly larger size to accommodate potential maximum entries for a field. Overestimating the size won't cause issues, but underestimating it may lead to the need for editing field properties in the table later, which can be cumbersome depending on the project's progress.

Understanding normal forms

Organizing tables to avoid data repetition or duplicated fields is known as normalization. There are five guidelines, called forms, to arrange data into non-repetitive tables. The first two forms are crucial for newcomers to database development, while the last three cater to more advanced users. Let's focus on the first two forms.

- **No duplicate columns:** A table shouldn't contain two fields like Zip and ZipCode holding the same information. However, it could be more efficient even if you have a field called CityStateZip that combines City, State, and Zip for convenience. Updating this combined field along with individual City, State, and Zip fields leads to duplicate data entry and violates the first normal form.

- **Put duplicate data in a child table:** The second normal form builds upon the first and advises placing duplicate information in a new child table. For instance, it may seem okay initially if you collect multiple phone numbers for volunteers (work, home, cell) and have separate fields for each in the Volunteers table. However, as your needs evolve, this approach becomes impractical. Instead, follow the second normal form and create a child table, like VolunteerPhone, with fields such as PhoneID, PhoneType, and PhoneNumber. It allows for easier addition of more phone numbers for each volunteer and simplifies querying data without needing to deal with multiple phone number fields.

Exploring the third through fifth normal forms will provide insightful articles and white papers for those interested in delving further into database normalization.

Normalizing your tables

By now, you've made excellent progress by specifying each field with its data type and size, and you've learned about the significance of table normalization and the first two normal forms. Now comes organizing your fields into tables, which might appear straightforward initially. However, as we've discussed earlier, there are better ways to go than creating just one table for all data.

To guide you in grouping fields into tables, follow these plain English principles:

- Ensure the data is related, sharing a common theme like volunteer contact information, events, or locations.

- Avoid repeating data. If you enter the same volunteer into the Volunteers table twice due to multiple addresses, it's time for a new table.

- Avoid using related choices as field names. Having separate volunteer fields in your events table, like Volunteer1, Volunteer2, and Volunteer3, poses querying challenges. Consider creating a new table if you need to specify multiple volunteers for an event.

Organize your field list by subject and check for duplicates based on the previous points. This process will result in a well-structured table layout.

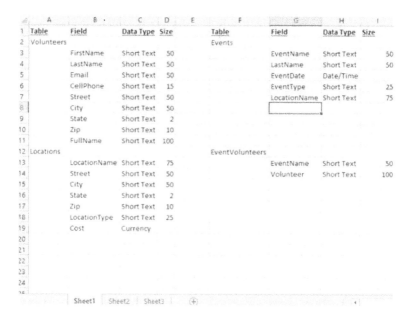

	A	B	C	D	E	F	G	H	I
1	Table	Field	Data Type	Size		Table	Field	Data Type	Size
2	Volunteers					Events			
3		FirstName	Short Text	50			EventName	Short Text	50
4		LastName	Short Text	50			LastName	Short Text	50
5		Email	Short Text	50			EventDate	Date/Time	
6		CellPhone	Short Text	15			EventType	Short Text	25
7		Street	Short Text	50			LocationName	Short Text	75
8		City	Short Text	50					
9		State	Short Text	2					
10		Zip	Short Text	10					
11		FullName	Short Text	100					
12	Locations					EventVolunteers			
13		LocationName	Short Text	75			EventName	Short Text	50
14		Street	Short Text	50			Volunteer	Short Text	100
15		City	Short Text	50					
16		State	Short Text	2					
17		Zip	Short Text	10					
18		LocationType	Short Text	25					
19		Cost	Currency						
20									
21									
22									
23									
24									

Sheet1 Sheet2 Sheet3 (+)

Don't keep adding fields if you need to accommodate future changes, like adding more volunteers to an event. Instead, create a new table called EventVolunteers, allowing flexibility in adding volunteers for each event.

Proper table design is crucial, especially when handling scenarios with multiple addresses per volunteer or numerous volunteers per event. This step ensures efficient querying and saves time and effort.

The importance of getting the table design right from the start becomes evident when comparing queries. For example, a query with ten volunteer fields would require repetitive entries and return unwanted results. On the other hand, normalized tables deliver cleaner results without unnecessary information. Designing your tables correctly initially will spare you from future frustration and difficulties.

Building Tables in Design View

With your data organized, it's time to create your tables. Here's how you can begin:

1. Open the Create tab on the Ribbon.

2. Click the Table Design button located in the Tables group.

You will be presented with a new table in Design view, all set for adding your new fields. Additionally, the Property Sheet and Field Properties will be visible. If you don't see the Property Sheet, press F4 to display it.

Creating fields

To save a table, it must contain at least one field. Since you've already organized your data into fields and tables beforehand (if not, refer to the section "Planning Your Database Tables" earlier in this chapter), this step should be straightforward.

Assuming you have a table open in Design View, follow these steps:

1. Click on the first empty row in the Field Name column.

2. Type your desired field name.

   Remember, a field name can have a maximum of 64 characters. It's best to keep the field names short and descriptive of the data they will store. It helps when referring to them in queries, forms, or reports since long field names mean more typing. Avoid using spaces in field names; if necessary, surround field names with square brackets ([]) that you must type. However, Access will automatically enter the square brackets if your field name lacks space.

3. In each subsequent blank row, type the field names that belong to your new table.

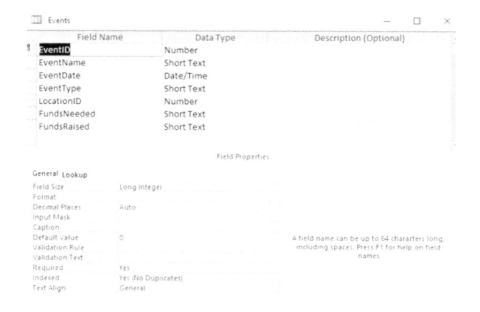

4. Choose File → Save (or press Ctrl+S) to save your new table.

As for table names, the maximum size is 64 characters. Similarly, it's advisable to keep table names short, avoid spaces, and steer clear of special characters. Stick to letters, numbers, and underscores (_) to prevent issues. If you need to differentiate words in your names, use underscores or capitalize the first letter of each word in your table name.

Setting data types

Once you've entered your field names, you need to specify the data they will hold by selecting an appropriate data type. Suppose you need clarification on data types and their selection. Follow these steps to assign data types to your fields:

1. Click in the Data Type column next to the new field.

   A drop-down list with various data type options will appear.

2. Select a suitable data type from the list.

3. If required, enter a field size on the Field Size property row in the Field Properties section of the Table Design view. Not all data types necessitate a field size, but most do.

4. Repeat Steps 2 and 3 for each field in the table.

5. Save the table.

Take your time building tables to ensure correctness from the start, as this will save you from future frustration and challenges.

Chapter 4: Types, Masks, and Triggers

Access Table Settings

Here's how to utilize five properties to maintain accurate data in your database:

- **Format:** Control the appearance of your data without altering its storage format.

- Input Mask: Enforce a specific data entry structure, like requiring phone numbers in the (###) ###-#### format.

- **Required:** Mandate data entry in a field before saving the record.

- **Validation Rule:** Specify rules for data in a field, such as requiring a number between 0 and 100.

- **Default Value:** Automatically enter data when inserting a new record.

All five properties can be accessed and modified in the Table Design view on the General tab within the Field Properties section. Follow these steps:

1. Open the database file containing the data you want to manage. Right-click the desired table from the Navigation pane, and choose Design View.

2. In the Design view, click the name of the field you wish to modify.

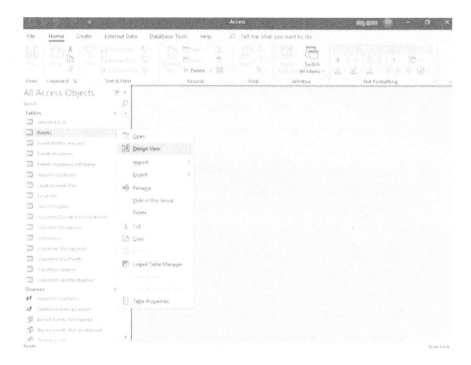

3. In the Field Properties section (the bottom half of the window), you'll find the Format, Input Mask, Default Value, Validation Rule, and Required boxes. Make the necessary changes in these boxes.

4. To save your changes, click the Save button on the Quick Access Toolbar.

Remember that the Validation Text box is connected to the Validation Rule box and complements its function. However, the steps provided here apply to all properties, regardless of which one you choose to apply.

Field Data Formats

Your database format presents data in a recognizable and clear arrangement on the screen. It alters the visual appearance of your data without affecting how it is stored in the table.

While formatting doesn't prevent inaccurate data entry, it can help identify data-entry errors more easily. Here's how formatting aids in reducing errors:

- **Enhances error visibility:** For instance, when typing the number one million into a numeric field, standard formatting displays it as 1,000,000 instead of 1000000, making it less prone to mistakes.

- **Reduces typing during data entry:** Text formatting can simplify data entry, like inputting a phone number 1112223333, while Access automatically displays it with parentheses and a dash.

Different field data types require distinct formatting codes. Text formatting uses different codes than numeric formatting. Refer to the following sections for formats suitable for the most common field data types.

If your format command doesn't work as expected, troubleshoot using these steps:

- **Double-check the data type:** If you encounter left-aligned numbers without a standard number of decimal places, you may have selected the Text data type for a numeric field. Changing the data type to Number or Currency will resolve this issue.

- **Review and modify format commands:** If you see percent signs but intend to display dollar signs, adjust the format from Percent to Currency using the Format Property drop-down list.

Text fields

In Access, text fields offer four characters to customize capitalization, spacing, and punctuation. Although Access lacks pre-designed formats for text fields, you can create your own by combining specific characters into a formatting string. This formatting string enables Access to display the text in a standardized manner according to your preferences.

Capitalization

Access presents text fields with their original capitalization as stored in the data. Nevertheless, Access offers the option to automatically display a field either in all uppercase or all lowercase letters, regardless of the stored data.

To modify the capitalization of an entire short text or long text field, adjust the Format property by using the greater-than or less-than symbol. This setting will influence how the field's text is presented in your database.

UPPERCASE

Using the greater-than symbol (>) in the Format box makes all the text within that field appear in uppercase, irrespective of how it was originally typed. This formatting option is handy for abbreviating U.S. state names, commonly represented in uppercase. However, it's important to note that this format does not alter how the text is stored. Therefore, you must apply the greater-than-symbol formatting each time the field appears on a form or report.

LOWERCASE

Using the less-than symbol (<) in the Format text box causes all the text within that field to appear lowercase, regardless of its original input. Type a single less-than symbol in the Format text box to apply this formatting option.

Spacing and punctuation

In Access, you can format the spacing and punctuation of typed text, allowing you to incorporate additional spaces or special characters, such as dashes.

A crucial reminder is to use the @ or & character in the format with care. Always include one @ or & to represent each typed character in the field. For instance, use @@ to denote two spaces and @@@ for three spaces. This approach ensures the accurate representation of the desired formatting in your data.

Number and currency fields

In Access, applying numeric formats to your numeric fields is made effortless. The software includes the seven most common formats in a convenient drop-down menu within the Format property row.

To set a format for a Number or Currency field, follow these steps:

1. While in the Design view of your table, click the Format text box corresponding to the field you wish to format.

2. Click the down arrow on the box's right side, and select the desired format for your field.

It's important to note that numeric formats only alter the appearance of the number, leaving the actual stored value unchanged. For instance, if you choose the Single Field Size and opt for the Standard format for a field containing 1.235678, you will see 1.24 on the screen, while Access retains the original value of 1.235678 in the field. Any calculations involving the numbers in that field will utilize the actual inputted value, not the formatted version visible on the screen.

The upcoming sections provide an overview of the numeric formats integrated into Access.

General Number format

The General Number format serves as the default in Access. When applied, it simply displays the data exactly as you entered it in the field without any alterations, including decimal places. Even if you format the number 1.23456 to General with two decimal places, it will still be displayed as 1.23456. Although it may seem counterintuitive, that's how this format operates in Access.

Currency format

The currency format transforms a regular number field to resemble a currency field, displaying the data as monetary.

Remember that numeric fields may or may not store decimal characters based on your chosen field size. Thus, decimal formatting becomes irrelevant if you opt for a field size that doesn't store decimal places, like Long Integer size.

Two currency formats are available to present data with two decimal places (representing "cents" in a dollar amount), using zeros when decimals are not initially present:

- **Currency:** Displays the local currency sign and appropriate punctuation, determined by Windows's Region & Language Settings.

The Currency formats don't automatically perform exchange-rate conversions for the selected currency. They display the chosen currency symbol preceding the value entered in the field.

Scientific, Percent, and Decimal formats

The remaining built-in formats serve various purposes, from presenting large numbers in scientific notation to displaying decimals as percentages:

- **Fixed:** Exhibits the decimal value without a comma as a thousand separator.

- **Standard:** Shows the decimal value with a thousand separator.

- **A tip for Fixed or Standard format:** You can adjust the number of decimal places displayed. By default, both formats round to two decimal places with the Auto setting. To specify a different number of decimal places, enter a value between 0 and 15 in the Decimal Places setting below the Format setting.

- **Percent:** This format appends a percent sign after the number.

- **Remember:** There is no need to convert percentages to decimals for data entry. To input 97%, type 97 in the field.

- If your percentages are only displayed as 0.00% or 100.00%, refer to the sidebar "What happened to my percentages?" for a solution.

- **Scientific:** Expresses numbers in scientific notation, indicating the first significant digits and the number of places these digits belong on the left or right side of the decimal point.

- **Technical information:** Scientific notation is primarily utilized for huge numbers (e.g., the distance light travels in a year) or tiny numbers (e.g., the distance light travels in a trillionth of a second) that are challenging to measure precisely or read quickly. It is best to only use this format if you are a scientist.

Date/time fields

Microsoft provides a drop-down menu full of ready-to-use date and time formats. Here's how to apply a date/time format to a field:

1. With your table in Design view, click the Format text box for the field you'd like to format.

2. Click the down arrow on the text box's right side.

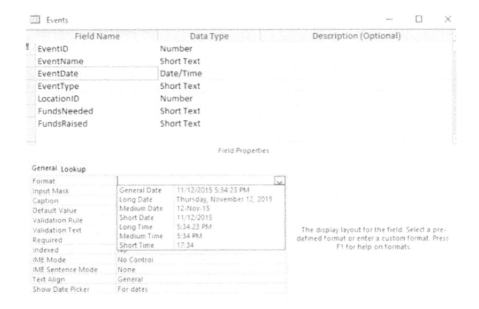

3. Select the format you want to use.

Yes/No fields

When it comes to fields with only three options, you can convey a limited amount of information. Strangely, Yes/No fields are automatically formatted as Yes/No by default.

If you prefer the flexibility to enter Yes/No, True/False, or On/Off in the field, ensure that the Display Control in the Lookup tab (next to the General tab) is set to Combo Box. Otherwise, the field will display check boxes, as Check Box is the default option for Yes/No fields.

Allowable Yes/No field entries

In a Yes/No field, you can enter the following options:

- Yes and No (this is the default)

- On and Off

- True and False

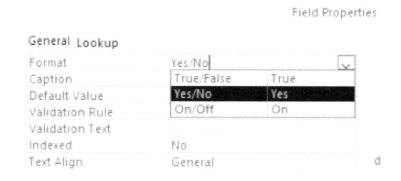

By default, the field displays Yes and No, but you can customize how a Yes/No field formats its content. Here's how to do it:

- Open your table in Design View.

- Click the Format text box for the field you want to format.

- Click the down arrow on the text box's right side.

- A menu with three Yes/No formats will appear, giving you options.

- Select the format you prefer from the menu.

If you wish to create custom choices instead of the standard Yes and No, type your personalized entry directly into the Format box. For instance, you can have something like:

- Agree and Disagree

- Positive and Negative

- Then, follow the same steps mentioned earlier to apply your custom format.

Gaining Control of Data Entry

To control data input effectively, you can use input masks, which consist of specific characters that dictate what kind of data is expected in a particular field. These masks prevent users from entering data that doesn't match the specified format. Input masks apply to Short Text, Number, Date/Time, and Currency field data types.

While formatting can make specific data-entry errors visible, it doesn't prevent such errors. On the other hand, input masks serve as a barrier to keep erroneous data out.

Access the Input Mask property box of the field's General tab to implement input masks. You can use masks for fields containing dates, times, phone numbers, Social Security numbers, passwords, zip codes, and other similar data. Using input masks, you'll avoid mistyped phone numbers (e.g., 111-123) and incorrect zip codes (e.g., 0854).

Input masks are most effective when dealing with short, consistent data, such as numbers and alphanumeric combinations that follow predictable patterns, like phone numbers, dates, and zip codes.

There are two ways to create an input mask:

- Use the Input Mask Wizard for assistance. Remember that the wizard may only cover some possible mask scenarios, primarily focusing on text and date fields, offering only a limited set of options.

- Manually construct the mask when dealing with data that follows a consistent pattern not covered by the Input Mask Wizard, such as a six-digit part number or similar formats.

Using the Input Mask Wizard

The Input Mask Wizard is readily available to assist you in creating masks for text fields (like phone numbers, Social Security numbers, and U.S. zip codes) or simple date and time fields.

If your data doesn't match the masks provided by the wizard but follows a consistent pattern, you can manually create a mask, as explained in the next section.

To use the wizard, follow these steps:

1. Open the database file with the data you wish to mask. Right-click on the table you want to modify and choose Design View.

2. Click on the field name where you want to apply the input mask. Please note that the wizard is compatible only with text and date/time fields.

3. Click the Input Mask box, and a Builder button will appear to the right.

4. Click the Builder button, and the wizard will show a selection of input masks.

Input Mask Wizard

Which input mask matches how you want data to look?

To see how a selected mask works, use the Try It box.

To change the Input Mask list, click the Edit List button.

Input Mask:	Data Look:
Long Time	1:12:00 PM
Short Date	9/27/1969
Short Time	13:12
Medium Time	01:12 PM
Medium Date	27-Sep-69

Try It: [__/__/____]

Edit List	Cancel	< Back	Next >	Finish

5. Scroll through the list and choose the input mask that suits your requirements.

6. You can test the mask by clicking the Try It area, typing a sample entry, and observing how it behaves.

7. Click Finish to close the wizard and apply the selected mask to your field.

If you click Next instead of Finish, the wizard will provide more options, but it's generally recommended to avoid them.

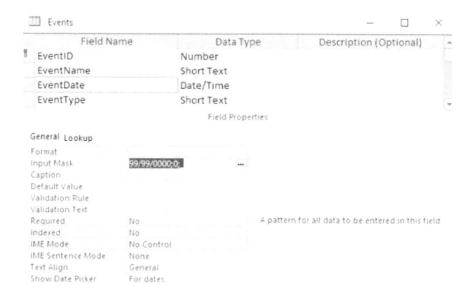

Once you finish using the wizard, the chosen mask will appear in the Input Mask text box in the Field Properties section of the table.

Making a mask by hand

The Input Mask Wizard may not offer the specific mask you require. But if you can concoct a seemingly random sequence of characters, then you have the power to create your input mask. The challenge lies in deciphering the meaning behind these seemingly nonsensical characters.

There are collections of codes that you can utilize in an input mask, each with an explanation of the characters it represents:

- **Required Code:** Users must input the specified type of character, whether they intend to or not.

- **Optional Code:** Users can input or omit the indicated character type mentioned in the first column. For instance, with an input mask like 99/99/0000;0;_, you can input 1/1/2023 or 01/01/2023, but 1/1/23 is not allowed.

Give Your Fingers a Mini Vacation by Default

Wouldn't it be fantastic if each time you added a new volunteer, you didn't have to enter the current date in the Start Date field manually? Hold on to your excitement because Access is here to fulfill your data-entry dreams! It achieves this magical feat through the Default Value property. By setting a Default Value, you can specify data for a field that will automatically populate each time a new record is added to the table. Yes, it may sound too good to be true, but trust me, it's a real feature!

To set a Default Value, follow these steps:

- Open the database file and right-click on the table you wish to work with. Choose Design View from the menu, and the table will switch to Design View.

- Click on the name of the field you want to modify.

- Click on the Default Value box.

- Type the data to appear in that field whenever a new record is added.

- Switch to Datasheet view by clicking the View button on the Ribbon, and then test your work.

- Give it a quick test: Add a new record and observe the field's contents that contain the default value you just set. You'll see the magic in action!

CHAPTER 5: A FORM FOR ALL REASONS

Generating Forms

You can create forms based on your requirements:

- **Form tools:** Generate visually appealing forms with a single mouse click.

- **Form Wizard:** Asks questions and then constructs an attractive form based on your responses.

- **Form Design and Blank Form buttons:** Allow you to initiate with an empty form and develop it from scratch.

Both the Form tools and Form Wizard simplify the form creation process. I focus on these two methods for building forms. The process of crafting forms entirely from scratch using a Design or Layout view falls beyond the scope of this book.

The Form Wizard and Form tools are time-saving offerings from Microsoft. Utilize them to construct your forms. They handle the intricate aspects, leaving you to add the final touches.

Here's how to decide which form-building approach to use:

- Opt for the Form tools if:

  - You want all fields from the chosen table or query to be on the form.

○ You're not concerned about controlling the style applied to the form.

○ Choose the Form Wizard if:

- You wish to pick particular fields for your form.

- You intend to select fields from multiple tables or queries.

- You want to choose from an assortment of layouts for your form.

Form tools

Here's the scoop on these tools, with a mix of good and not-so-good news. The positive side is that they're speedy and don't involve questioning or back-and-forth interactions! And the Flip side is that They're notably rigid in their functionality.

You're on your own if you're seeking a bigger font or a different background color. The Form tools make the decisions regarding font, colors, and layout.

To craft a form using one of the Form tools, launch your database and adhere to these steps:

- In the Navigation pane, choose the table or query containing the data you want your new form to showcase.

- Click on the Create tab located in the Ribbon.

- The Ribbon will exhibit several button groups, including the Forms group.

- Select the form button you prefer from the Forms group.

- The Simple Form button is titled "Form." The Multiple Items and Split Form buttons can be accessed via the More Forms drop-down list.

In an instant, a visually appealing form will materialize before you.

To finalize your form, follow these steps:

- Click the Save button on the Quick Access Toolbar.

- The Save As dialog box will appear.

- Enter a name for the form within the dialog box and click "OK."

- Your form's name will appear in the Navigation pane.

- Meeting your preferences: The Form Wizard

- When overseeing field selection and customizing form design, turn to the Form Wizard.

As with other Access wizards, the Form Wizard guides you step by step through the creation process. To utilize the Form Wizard, follow these instructions:

- Open your database file.

- Click on the Create tab in the Ribbon.

- Various button groups will emerge in the Ribbon, including the Forms group.

- Click the Form Wizard button.

- The Form Wizard will make its appearance, ready for action.

Employ the Tables/Queries drop-down menu to designate the source of the form's fields:

- Click the down arrow to unveil the database's tables and queries.

- Select the relevant table or query containing the fields you wish to display in this form.

- The Form Wizard will list the available fields.

- Choose the specific fields you want:

- Double-click each desired field in the Available Fields list for individual field selection.

- To include all fields from your table or query in the form, click the >> button in the middle of the screen.

- Once you've selected the fields you wish to incorporate in your form, proceed by clicking the "Next" button.

For those interested in the technical aspects: If you've picked fields from multiple tables, the Form Wizard will pause momentarily to inquire about how you intend to structure the data in your form. If you opt to arrange your data by the parent table, you'll be prompted to display child table data in either of two ways:

- **Subform:** This displays data from both tables within a single form.

- **Linked form:** This generates a button that, when clicked, leads you to a new form showcasing the child table data.

When the wizard prompts you for the form layout, choose from the following options and then proceed by clicking "Next":

- **Columnar:** Displays records individually, one at a time.

- **Tabular:** Displays multiple records simultaneously with an appealing form style.

- **Datasheet:** Exhibits multiple records simultaneously in a less visually pleasing, spreadsheet-like format.

- **Justified:** Arrange form fields neatly in rows, accentuated with prominent left and right margins.

- At the top of the Form Wizard screen, provide a descriptive title in the "What Title Do You Want for Your Form?" box.

- Before concluding the Form Wizard, tailor your new form by selecting the "Modify the form's design" radio button. If you prefer to preview it first, stick with the default choice ("Open the form to view or enter information"), which opens the form in Form view.

- With the setup complete, click "Finish" to unveil the form in Form view.

- Your fresh form will materialize on the screen.

- The Form Wizard automatically saves the form as part of its creation process. You needn't manually save or name it. All saved forms will be accessible within the Forms section of the Navigation pane.

Customizing Form Parts

The Access Form tools and Form Wizard excel at constructing forms, handling a wide range of tasks for most users. Nevertheless, there are instances where they may need to catch up, necessitating some manual form adjustments.

With a grasp of fundamental form design principles, you can address most issues left unresolved by the Form tools and Form Wizard.

This segment illustrates how to modify the overall aesthetics of the form. Specifically, it guides you in gaining control over tasks such as relocating, resizing, labeling, and formatting controls within your forms. (A control refers to any design component on a form, such as a line, label, or data-entry box, which influences the form's appearance.)

Taking the Layout view

Form-design alterations can be made in either the Design or Layout view. Refer to the "A form with a view" sidebar for insights into these perspectives.

These guidelines primarily focus on the Layout view due to its user-friendly nature.

To access Layout view, adhere to these steps:

- Right-click on the form you wish to modify within the Navigation pane.

  A context menu will emerge.

- Select "Layout View" from the context menu.

Styling with a Theme

Following the creation of your new form through the Form Wizard or Form tools, you might find yourself dissatisfied with the chosen appearance. Fear not! Altering the form's aesthetics is a breeze, thanks to the Theme group of buttons. Here's how:

- Right-click on the form requiring a new look from the Navigation pane.

- Opt for "Layout View" from the emerging menu.

- The form will open in the Layout view.

- Click on the Design tab located in the Ribbon.

- The Ribbon will display several button groups, including the Themes group.

- Click the Themes button.

- A visual list (termed a Gallery) of themes will unfold.

- Slowly hover your mouse pointer over each theme.

- The background form will alter its appearance to match the highlighted theme.

- Once you've pinpointed a theme you fancy, click on it to select it from the drop-down list and apply it to the form.

- Select a theme with legible fonts and soothing colors, such as gentle hues and straightforward fonts. Users of the form will appreciate this consideration!

Managing form controls

A control is any design element (such as a line, label, or data-entry text box) that appears on a form. The Form Wizard and Form tools do a fine job constructing forms but often don't place or size them just right. This section discusses how to take charge of your controls.

Control types

The two primary control types have distinct functions: showcase data extracted from an underlying table or query (such as a text box) or contribute design elements to maintain data organization on the form (like a line).

These are the prevalent form controls you encounter:

- **Text box:** The area where you input your data.

- Text boxes are linked (bound) to a table field or independent (unbound), potentially containing calculations derived from other fields within a table.

- **Label:** The explanatory text adjacent to the control or the form's title.

- **Combo box:** A dropdown list presenting various choices.

- **List box:** A container housing a list of choices, allowing users to select multiple items.

- **Check box:** A square box linked to a field that holds true/false, on/off, or yes/no responses. For instance, consider a personnel table featuring a "Married" field. It's either a yes or a no.

- **Option Group:** A box encompassing related choices, permitting only one selection. For instance, suppose a "Marital Status" field includes choices like Married,

Single, and Divorced. An option group control linked to that field would allow just one of these choices.

- **Subform:** A form embedded within another form.

  Subforms generally showcase the "many" records associated with the "one" record in scenarios where tables exhibit a one-to-many relationship.

In the case of a columnar form (which is common), crafted using the Form Wizard or Form tools, all text boxes and labels within the form are anchored. Anchored controls behave collectively when resized. Additionally, you can relocate anchored controls within the group of other controls, but not if they're positioned outside the group.

Creating controls

Most controls are equipped with a Control Wizard that accompanies their creation. After you've established the control, the wizard emerges to guide the process. The following are the basic steps for forming a control:

- Begin by right-clicking on the form in the Navigation pane where you intend to add the new control and select "Design View."

  If needed, navigate to the Design tab on the Ribbon.

- This action unveils the control group.

- Choose the desired control type (like a combo box) from the Controls group, and hover the mouse pointer over the form.

- The mouse cursor transforms into a plus sign combined with the icon of the chosen control.

- Place the mouse at the desired spot on the form where you wish to introduce the new control. Then, press and drag diagonally to define the control's dimensions.

- If applicable, the Control Wizard will make an appearance.

- If the chosen control involves a Control Wizard, follow the Control Wizard's steps and conclude by clicking "Finish."

- The control will now materialize on the form.

Managing Data in Form View

Your form design is complete, and you're all set to test it out. This portion elucidates navigating between records, initiating new records, and more.

Navigating and finding records

How can you transition between records on the form? Utilize the Navigation buttons positioned at the form's lower left corner. These buttons provide a convenient way to:

- **Navigate among records:** Utilize the right arrowhead (>) for moving forward, the left arrowhead (<) for moving backward, the right arrowhead with a line (>|) for accessing the last record, and the left arrowhead with a line (<|) for returning to the first record.

- **Initiate a new record:** Click the right arrowhead with an asterisk (>*) button to proceed to a new record.

- **Search for specific data:** Enter a search term in the Search box, and Access will promptly locate the first record containing that search term. For instance, if you type "Prince" into the Search box, Access will efficiently navigate to the first record with the term "Prince."

Saving, clearing, and deleting

The transition from the Word and Excel environment to Access can be perplexing. In most other applications, entering new content into a document and clicking "Save" preserves your work. However, Access operates differently. The moment you switch to a new record or close a form, Access automatically saves the record. This distinct approach significantly reduces the chances of data loss in Access. While erasing field data and deleting records is slightly less automatic, this design is beneficial.

For those who lean towards extra caution, it's possible to save a record before leaving it or closing the form. You can do this by clicking the "Save" button found in the Records group of the

Home Ribbon. Alternatively, pressing Ctrl+S on your keyboard achieves the same result.

Visual depiction of record selectors and the frequently used Records group on the Home Ribbon.

To clear the content from a field, follow these steps:

- In Form view, navigate to the field containing undesired data.

- The contents of the field will be highlighted.

- Press the Delete key on your keyboard.

- The contents of the field will be erased.

Here's how to delete an entire record:

- While in Form view, locate the record you wish to delete.

- Click on the Record Selector button on the form's left side.

- Proceed to click "Delete" and then "Delete Record" within the Records group on the Ribbon Home tab.

- Access will inquire whether you want to delete the record along with related records if appropriate.

- Confirm the action by clicking "Yes" to remove the record in the confirmation dialog box.

CHAPTER 6: IMPORTING AND EXPORTING DATA

Retrieving Data from Other Sources

Access offers two methods to bring data from other applications into your database:

- **Importing:** This feature enables you to convert data from an external format into the Access database file format and then incorporate it into an Access table. There are two ways to import data:

  1. Create a new table in an Access database for the imported data. This option is suitable when building a new database; some data is already available in spreadsheets or other formats.

  2. Append the data as new records at the end of an existing table. This method is useful when you need to import monthly expense data into your expense reporting database from your credit card company, and the data is provided in spreadsheet format.

- **Linking:** This approach establishes a temporary connection between the external data and Access. The data remains in its source, but Access can manipulate it as if it were residing within the source, often another Access database. Once a link is created, it persists until you delete it or the source file is moved or removed.

When you link tables between two Access databases, you cannot modify the structure of the source table directly in the destination database (the database containing the links). It would help if you opened the source database to edit the table structure linked to the destination database.

Spreadsheets

During the import of a spreadsheet file into Access, each column in the spreadsheet corresponds to a field in the Access table:

- The first row of the spreadsheet, which contains the column headings, becomes the field names in Access.

- If you wish to use the first row as field names, you should ensure to check the "First Row Contains Column Headings" checkbox during the import process.

- An ideal spreadsheet for import should have its field names in Row 1.

- Subsequent rows in the spreadsheet become individual records in the Access table.

- An ideal spreadsheet for import should have its data starting from Row 2.

- When importing data from spreadsheets, be cautious of the following nuances:

- Verify the consistency and completeness of the spreadsheet data.

- Ensure that each entry in every spreadsheet column (field) has the same data type (e.g., numbers, text).

- Remove titles and blank rows from the top of the spreadsheet to prevent interference during import.

- Keep your spreadsheet column headings concise and distinct.

- Adjust your spreadsheet column headings to match the field names you want to use in Access to avoid import issues related to field names.

- If you add data to an existing Access table, ensure the spreadsheet columns are in the same number and order as the Access table fields.

- Your spreadsheet columns must align perfectly with the corresponding table fields in Access.

Text files

If you encounter difficulties importing a particular format, like an Excel spreadsheet, into Access, you might consider importing the data as text. Text is a universally recognized data format understood by both humans and computers. Follow these steps to import the data as text:

- Please open the file using the software product it was created in, such as Excel.

- Utilize the existing software's exporting tools or the "Save As" command to export the data into a text file.

- Exporting the data as a delimited text file is preferable if the existing software supports this format. In a delimited file, each field is separated by a marker character, like a comma, allowing Access to distinguish where one field ends and the next begins.

- Proceed to import the text file into Access (as demonstrated later in this chapter).

Importing and linking

When deciding between linking and importing data in Access, consider the specific situation:

- **Linking:** Use this method if the data in the other program must remain in that program. For instance, if the data is stored in an SQL Server database as a permanent business fixture, linking to the source is the way to go.

- **Importing:** Choose importing if you want the database where you place the data to replace the source. This option is suitable when creating an Access database to replace an old spreadsheet that no longer meets your needs. Additionally, import data if it comes from an external vendor in a format other than Access. For example, if you receive monthly historical trend data in spreadsheet format from an outside vendor, importing it into Access allows you to leverage powerful reporting tools for generating reports.

Importing

To import or link data sources to your Access database, follow these steps:

1. Open the Access database where you want to store the imported data.

2. Click on the External Data tab located on the Ribbon.

   The Import & Link group of buttons is displayed on the Ribbon.

3. Click the New Data Source button to access a list of data source categories, such as From File and Database.

4. Choose the appropriate category as explained in the "Translating data formats" section earlier in this chapter.

   A Get External Data dialog box specific to the selected file format will appear on the screen.

5. Use the Browse button to select the data source you want to import or link to Access. It can be a file, website, or an Outlook folder.

6. Select the method of data storage, indicating whether you want to import or link the data. Note that you can link to most data formats except XML.

7. Follow the remaining steps in the Get External Data dialog box. The subsequent steps will depend on your importing data format, so follow the prompts carefully. Double-check the source file's format if you encounter gibberish in the imported or linked table. For instance, if it's a text file, ensure it was saved as

Troubleshooting

While importing or linking data, Access might encounter some issues that become apparent through either a prolonged process or an error message display. This section covers common problems that may arise during the import or linking process and provides solutions to address these issues.

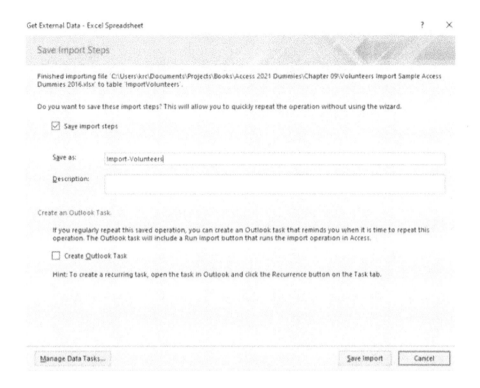

Slow imports and links

If importing takes an extended time, it's likely due to errors in the inbound data. Follow these steps to troubleshoot the issue:

- Press Ctrl+Break to halt the import process.

- If your device lacks a Break key, refer to its documentation for the proper key sequence to implement the Break command. For instance, it might be the Fn+F6 key combination on some laptops, so you'd press Ctrl+Fn+F6 to stop the import process.

Open the source file in its original application and examine the data being imported for problems, such as:

- **Corrupt data:** The file you're trying to import could be damaged and unusable.

- Disorganized spreadsheet data

- **Invalid index:** Sometimes, database indexes become corrupt, making the data within the table with the invalid index unusable. Access will usually alert you when you open the invalid index source table.

Make any necessary corrections and save the corrected source file.

Export formats

Access allows you to export data to various formats, including Excel, Text, XML, SharePoint, ODBC, HTML, and dBASE (as listed earlier in this chapter). Additionally, you can export to PDF (Adobe Acrobat files), XPS (XML Paper Specification), Microsoft Word, and as an email attachment.

Exporting table or query data is a straightforward process:

1. Open the database and select the table or query you wish to export from the Navigation pane.

2. Click the External Data tab on the Ribbon to access the Export button group.

The Export button group offers dedicated buttons for common exporting tasks, and the More button provides access to less frequently used formats.

3. Choose the appropriate button corresponding to the program you intend to export your data to.

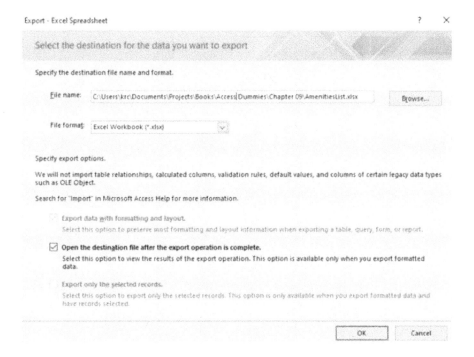

4. An Export dialog box tailored to your chosen format will appear, allowing you to proceed with the export.

5. Choose the Save Export Steps check box if you plan on exporting again.

CHAPTER 7: ACCESS AND THE WEB

How Access Works with the Web Using the Access Web Browser Control

The web browser control enables you to embed a web page within an Access form or report. This allows you to showcase your client's website, launch a search engine, or present any desired web content. Simply input the web page's address, and you can even link the control to a form/report field containing the web page address.

Imagine you have a form showcasing client information, including a field named "WebAddress" for the client's website. By linking Access's web browser control to this field, the control will dynamically display the website corresponding to the record being viewed. Here's how to proceed:

1. Access the Design view of the form where you want to integrate web page data.

2. Go to the Design tab on the Ribbon and click on the Web Browser Control tool.

3. Starting from the upper left corner of your desired display area on the form, drag out a sizable box and release the mouse button.

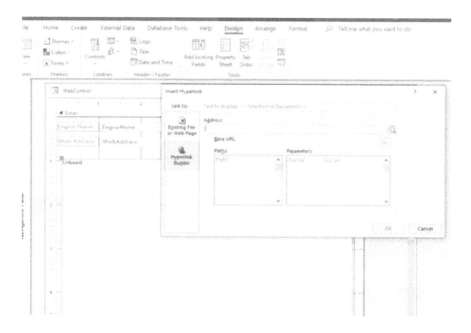

4. The Insert Hyperlink dialog box will appear. If you want the same web page to be displayed regardless of the record, input the web page address in the Address box.

5. To link the web browser control to a web page address stored in a table field, close the Insert Hyperlink dialog box by clicking Cancel. Then, access the Property Sheet in the Tools group under the Design tab on the Ribbon.

While the web browser control is selected, navigate to the Data tab in the Property Sheet. Set the control source property to the field name containing the web page address.

View the form in Form view. Observe the web browser control dynamically showing the web page from Step 5 within the designated field.

Switch between records on the form.

You'll notice that the web browser control updates to display the specific web page corresponding to the selected record. While this process is intriguing, it's important to keep moving forward.

Using hyperlinks in your desktop Access database

Establishing a connection between your desktop database and the external world is a straightforward process. You're likely acquainted with the term "hyperlink" — it refers to text or images functioning as gateways to other data. When you click a hyperlink, you're directed to a different web page. Clicking an image configured as a hyperlink (indicated by the mouse pointer transforming into a pointing finger) leads you to an enlarged version of the image or to an alternate website containing information relevant to the image's subject. Underlined text or text changing color upon pointing are indications of a hyperlink's presence.

But what exactly is this "hyperlink"? Despite its energetic name, in the context of Access, it serves as a designated storage space for holding the address of a resource on the Internet, your local corporate network, or a file stored on your computer. Hyperlinks begin with a unique identification code that instructs the computer about the type of resource it points to and its location.

To delve deeper into links and Access's utilization of them, press F1 or type "Help" in the "tell me what you want to do" box (found to the right of the last tab name on the Ribbon). This opens the Access Help system, where you can search for the term "hyperlink data type."

If you're a frequent web surfer, many of these concepts and terms might be familiar. While numerous are designed for internet or intranet applications, Access can also leverage hyperlinks to identify documents stored locally (as demonstrated by "file://"). This empowers you to create hyperlinks in your Access table that open Word documents, Excel spreadsheets, or JPEG image files. The adaptability of this technology knows no bounds.

Adding a Hyperlink field to your desktop database table

Access offers a specialized field type tailored for this unique category of information. As you may have already deduced, this category is referred to as the Hyperlink field.

Incorporating a Hyperlink field into a table doesn't necessitate any distinct procedures. Simply follow the same steps as you would for adding any field to a table. Access the Design view of your table and utilize the Data Type column to select the Hyperlink data type.

The process of applying the Hyperlink data type is no different from dealing with other field types. When you return to

Datasheet view, you'll notice that your entries (if any) within the Hyperlink field are underlined, resembling link text on a web page.

To alternate between the Design and Datasheet views of your data, click the View button located on the Home tab or the Design tab of the Ribbon. This button, which is the first one, appears either as:

A table icon (depicting a small grid) or an icon amalgamating images of a ruler and an angle.

Fine-tuning your hyperlinks

After setting up your hyperlink field, input your hyperlinks using the Edit Hyperlink menu. Follow these steps to input a hyperlink:

1. While viewing your table in Datasheet mode, right-click on the desired Hyperlink field that you wish to modify within your table.

2. Choose the "Hyperlink" option and then select "Edit Hyperlink" from the context menu.

   A smart and compact dialog box will appear.

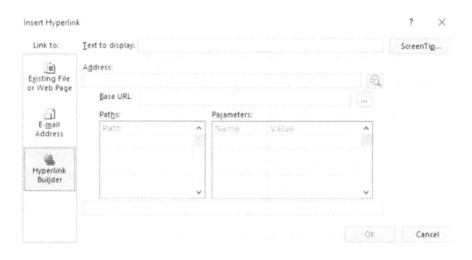

3. Utilize this dialog box to provide the following details:

    - The text to be displayed.

    - The ScreenTip (a brief text that emerges when your mouse pointer hovers over a web address). To create one, click the ScreenTip button and utilize the ensuing "Set Hyperlink ScreenTip" dialog box to formulate your tip. Click "OK" to return to the "Edit Hyperlink" dialog box.

    - Links for documents, spreadsheets, graphics, or even email addresses in an Access database.

    - The website address.

4. Click "OK."

This edit will modify your hyperlink, presenting the chosen display text and directing to the designated web address, document, or other file. If you've chosen to create a ScreenTip, you can test the new tip in Datasheet view by moving your mouse over the hyperlink to see what appears.

Pretty neat, isn't it? Play around with the dialog box a bit to explore its functionality. It takes only a brief moment.

Keep in mind that although most hyperlinks typically store web or Internet addresses, they can point to various elements in the digital realm. Thanks to their adaptable tags, hyperlinks can comprehend web pages, intranet servers, database components (such as reports and forms), as well as documents on your computer or other network-connected PCs.

Testing links

Hyperlinks within your table function similarly to those encountered on the internet — a simple point and click action. You can verify this yourself by following these steps:

- Ensure you're connected to the internet.

- It's important to note that when a hyperlink directing to a website is clicked, your default browser (like Edge) will open. However, if you're not online at that moment, the hyperlink won't direct you to its intended destination.

- Open the Access desktop database you wish to utilize.

- Access the table containing the hyperlinks.

- Click on the hyperlink you prefer.

- If the hyperlink directs you to a web page, your web browser will launch, showcasing the website linked to.

- In case the hyperlink leads to something other than a website, Windows will automatically activate the appropriate program to manage the content associated with the link. For instance, if it's an Excel document hyperlink, Excel will be launched to handle it.

Publishing Access objects to the web

Merely embedding web content within your tables, forms, or reports isn't the final point of connection between Access and the Internet. You have the option to convert your Access objects into HTML documents, allowing you to upload them to a web server, making them accessible online to a global audience.

To prepare your objects for publishing on a website, follow these steps:

1. Open the database containing the object intended for the web.

   The Access interface will be prominently displayed.

2. In the Navigation pane positioned on the left side of the window, select the specific object you wish to preserve as an HTML document.

The chosen object will be highlighted in the Navigation pane.

If your aim is to publish particular records from a table, create a query that isolates those records, and then select the query in the Navigation pane rather than the table itself.

3. Right-click on the selected object and opt for the "Export" option.

   A list of available Export types, including the standard ones, will emerge.

4. Choose "HTML Document" from the list.

   This action opens the "Export – HTML Document" dialog box. The current object's location and file name will be visible in the "File Name" text box, with the object's file extension altered to .html.

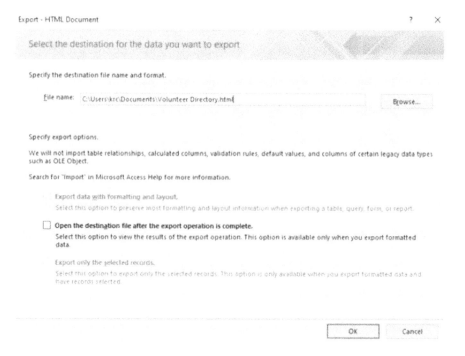

5. If necessary, click the "Browse" button to establish the folder location and the file name for the impending publication.

6. The Export – HTML Document dialog box presents three choices, and the availability of options may vary based on the type of object you intend to export.

   These three options are as follows:

   - Export Data with Formatting and Layout.

   - Open the Destination File after Export Operation is Complete.

- Export Only the Selected Records (this is accessible if you've chosen one or more records in the table prior to initiating this process)

7. Click the checkbox for "Open the Destination File after Export Operation is Complete."

8. Click the "OK" button.

9. This action triggers another dialog box titled "HTML Output Options."

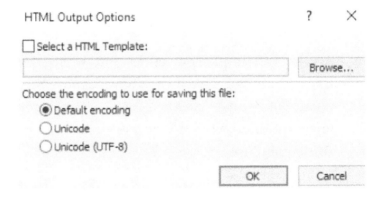

10. Select an appropriate HTML output option and click "OK":

- If you lack an HTML template and simply want the object to display in a browser window, click "OK."

- If you do possess a template in the form of an existing HTML document, mark the "Select a HTML Template" checkbox. Then, hit the

"Browse" button to navigate to the template, providing Access with its location. In the subsequent "HTML Template to Use" dialog box, you can return to the Export HTML Document dialog by selecting your desired template file and clicking "OK."

- There's no need to fret over the encoding method, so accept the "Default Encoding" option.

11. Finally, click "Close."

The Export HTML Document dialog box will close.

Access will inquire whether you want to save your Export settings. Leave the "Save Export Steps" option unchecked and click "Close." The procedure is uncomplicated, with no unique steps to be retained for subsequent use.

12. Now, open your web browser and observe your new HTML document.

Your object will appear within the browser window. Forms and reports should resemble their appearance in Access. Tables and queries will manifest as grids. If you chose to open the destination file after the export operation is complete, a browser window will automatically open, showcasing your new HTML document.

In case you didn't opt for the "Open the Destination File after Export Operation is Complete" option, you'll need to recall where you saved the file.

At this stage, all that remains is to upload your HTML document to either of these two locations:

- Your internal intranet server

- A web server for worldwide access

For this, you'll need FTP software (FTP stands for File Transfer Protocol). The software ensures your upload adheres to the guidelines for uploading documents to servers. You'll also need the login details for the server where your document will be stored. Once uploaded, you can view it online by entering the URL (web address) of the website containing your HTML document into any browser's address bar.

Numerous shareware and freeware versions of FTP software can be found. Just search for "FTP software" on your preferred search engine. If you're uploading files to your company's intranet or web server, you'll likely receive IT-approved software and instructions on how and where to upload your files.

CONCLUSION

Microsoft Access is a potent tool for managing databases and catering to businesses, students, and individuals' needs. Throughout this guide, we've gotten into Access's numerous functions and capabilities, ranging from creating tables and queries to designing forms and reports.

We've furnished practical instances and step-by-step guidance to aid you in becoming proficient with Access, enhancing your efficiency and effectiveness.

Access empowers you to arrange, retain, and dissect data in a streamlined and impactful manner. Whether overseeing finances, monitoring project advancement, or crafting interactive forms and reports, Access encompasses all the necessary tools to accomplish your tasks.

This guide has proven to be a valuable asset, aiding you in fully harnessing the potential of Microsoft Access. Always remember, the horizons of Access are boundless, so continue your journey of exploration, unearthing novel methods of working with data.

www.ingramcontent.com/pod-product-compliance
Lightning Source LLC
LaVergne TN
LVHW022125060326

832903LV00063B/4067